Contents

Some words are shown in bold, **like this**. You can find out what they mean by looking in the glossary.

World champions!

Football is the world's favourite sport. All over the world, footballers want to be the best. Many dream of lifting the World Cup for their country.

These South African children may play in the World Cup one day.

In 2010, the team from Spain won the World Cup.

Each team at the World Cup is from a different country. Teams come from every **continent**, apart from frozen Antarctica. The winners are the world **champions**.

The global game

Football is played in more than 200 different countries. Teams from the same **continent** play each other to see who will go to the World Cup finals competition. Only 32 countries get to play in the finals.

Teams from Honduras (in white) and Cuba play each other to try and reach the World Cup in 2014.

Ivory Coast's Yaya Toure (right in photo) plays for Manchester City in the Premier League.

Most of the time, footballers play for **football clubs**. In the World Cup, footballers play for the team from their **home country**.

World Cup history

Football became popular around the world about 100 years ago. Countries decided to hold a competition to find the world's best team. The first World Cup was held in Uruguay, South America, in 1930.

Uruguay were the first World Cup winners.

Brazil's team in 1970 was one of the World Cup's best ever teams.

Since 1930, the World Cup has been played every four years, except for 1942 and 1946 when it was cancelled. Brazil has won the World Cup five times – more than any other team.

The host country

A different country is chosen to **host** each World Cup. The teams play their matches in huge **stadiums**. **Fans** fill the stadiums to support their team.

This stadium was specially built for the 2010 World Cup in South Africa.

South African performers celebrate the opening ceremony at the 2010 World Cup.

The World Cup begins with an amazing opening ceremony. Musicians and dancers welcome players and fans to the festival of football.

The biggest stars

At the World Cup, football's biggest stars can show off their **skills**. Players can become famous around the world if they play well in the World Cup.

Portugal's Cristiano Ronaldo (left in photo) is one of the world's most famous footballers.

England's Gary Lineker (left in photo) won the Golden Boot at the 1986 World Cup.

The best player at each World Cup is given the Golden Ball award. The player who scores the most goals wins a golden football boot!

Women's World Cup

Women's football has its own World Cup. The first Women's World Cup was held in China in 1991. Since then, more and more people have started to play and watch women's football.

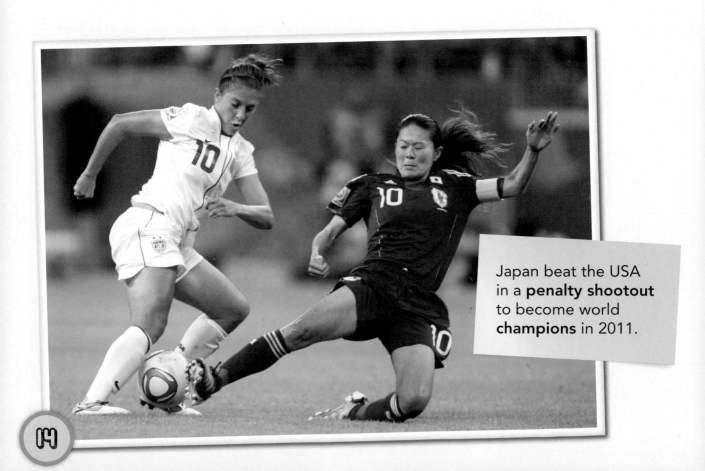

Japan beat the USA in a **penalty shootout** to become world **champions** in 2011.

Canada's Christine Sinclair will be cheered on by the **fans** at the Women's World Cup in Canada.

In 2015, Canada will **host** the Women's World Cup. Matches will be played in six cities across the country. Twenty-four teams will battle on the pitch to be world champions.

Terrific teams

Football is a team game. Eleven players play in each team. At the start of every World Cup match, they sing their country's **national anthem**.

Teams from Brazil and Scotland line up to sing their national anthems.

Nigeria's goalkeeper dives to save the ball in a match against Greece during the 2010 World Cup.

Every team needs a goalkeeper and defenders. Their job is to stop the other team from scoring a goal.

Silky skills

Even the world's best players have to practise every day. They need to be able to **dribble** with the ball at their feet or kick long **passes** to their teammates.

The Italy team practise before the 2010 World Cup.

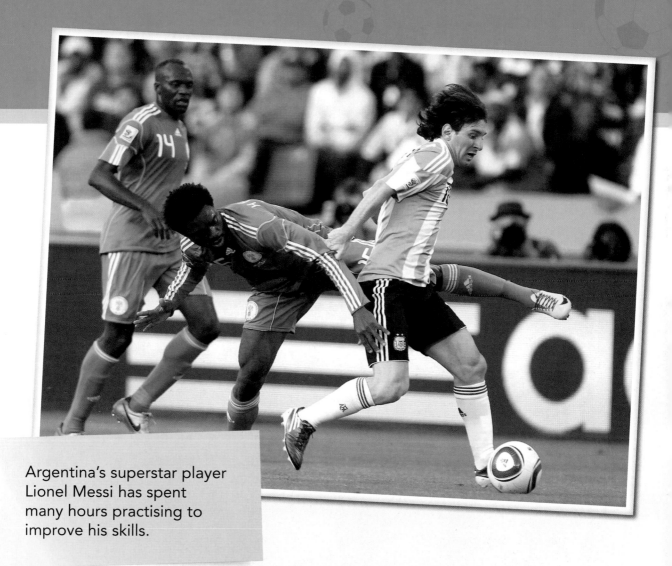

Argentina's superstar player Lionel Messi has spent many hours practising to improve his skills.

Playing at the World Cup makes all the practice worthwhile. Players can show their **skills** in front of thousands of **fans**. Millions more people watch on television.

A striker's job is to score goals. Some goals are scored with a great kick into the corner of the goal. Others are headed into the goal. Whichever way they are scored, they all count the same.

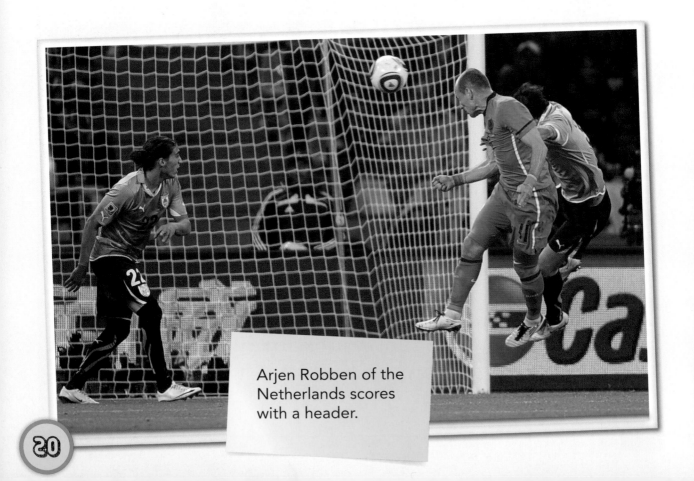

Arjen Robben of the Netherlands scores with a header.

Players from South Korea celebrate with their fans after scoring a goal.

The goal scorer celebrates with his team. The team's coaches and **fans** celebrate, too. One goal could be enough to win the match.

Fair play

Playing fairly is important in the World Cup. The referee is in charge. If a player breaks the rules, he can be shown a yellow card. A red card means he is sent off the pitch.

The referee's red card means that Uruguay's Luis Suarez is sent off the pitch.

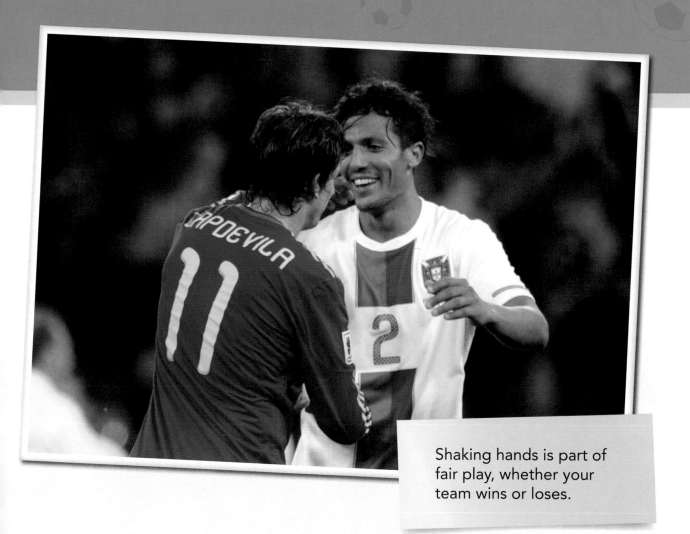

Shaking hands is part of fair play, whether your team wins or loses.

During the match, players try hard to beat the other team. At the end, they shake hands with their **opponents** and the referee. Sometimes they change shirts with the other team's players.

Winning and losing

To win the World Cup, teams have to play seven matches. First, they have to play three different teams in the **group stage**. After this, teams must win each match to go through to the next round.

Spain's players celebrate after reaching the 2010 World Cup final.

In a penalty shootout, each team takes five penalty shots at the goal.

If both teams have scored the same number of goals at the end of the last four matches, they play **extra time** to see if one team can win. If the score is still level, a **penalty shootout** decides the winner.

The world is watching

You don't have to be in the **stadium** to see the World Cup. **Fans** support their country's team and watch the matches on giant television screens or at home.

These Japanese fans are dressed up to support their team.

These fans are upset because Germany has been knocked out of the World Cup.

Every fan hopes that their country can win the World Cup this time. They are upset when their team loses. They have to wait four years for the next chance to win.

Welcome to Brazil

In 2014, the World Cup will go to Brazil in South America. Brazil is one of the world's biggest countries. It is home to over 190 million people. Brazilians love football.

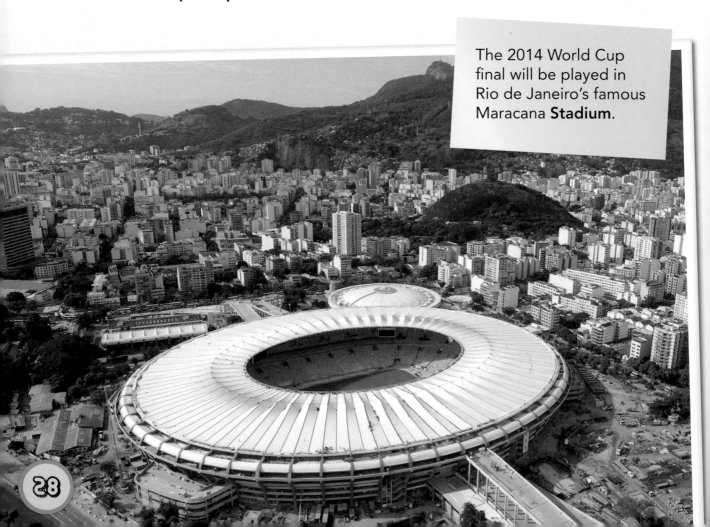

The 2014 World Cup final will be played in Rio de Janeiro's famous Maracana **Stadium**.

The stadiums will be filled with the sound of the Brazilian fans' drums.

Brazil has won the World Cup more times than any other team. Skilful Brazilian players are exciting to watch. Brazil is also home to some of the world's most **passionate** football **fans**.

World Cup facts

- The player who has scored the most goals at the World Cup is Brazil's Ronaldo, with 15 goals.

- England has won the World Cup just once, in 1966. In the same year, the World Cup was stolen. It was found by a dog called Pickles.

World Cup winners	
Year	Winners
1990	West Germany
1994	Brazil
1998	France
2002	Brazil
2006	Italy
2010	Spain

Women's World Cup winners	
Year	Winners
1991	USA
1995	Norway
1999	USA
2003	Germany
2007	Germany
2011	Japan

Glossary

champion someone who wins at a sport is called a champion

continent large area of land that is often split into several countries, such as Europe or Africa

dribble run with a football, keeping it close to your feet

extra time time added at the end of a drawn match to see if one team can score a winning goal

fan supporter of a football team

football club team that plays regularly in a league, including local teams and clubs that are made up of stars from across the world

group stage series of matches where groups of four or more teams play matches against each of the other teams in their group. The top one or two teams in each group go through to the next round.

home country country where you were born or which you think of as your home

host the World Cup's host country provides the stadiums and organization for the event

national anthem official song of a country

opponent players or team you are playing against

pass kick the football to another player on your own team

passionate having or showing strong emotions

penalty shootout way of deciding the winner if a match is still a draw at the end of extra time. Each team tries to score with penalty kicks.

skills ability to do different football moves, such as dribbling, passing, or shooting

stadium place where lots of people go to watch sport

Find out more

Books

Brazil (My Country), Annabel Savery
   (Franklin Watts, 2012)
Football World Cup, Clive Gifford (Ticktock, 2009)
Striker (Football Files), Michael Hurley (Raintree, 2010)

Website

www.fifa.com
Visit FIFA's website to find out everything you need
to know about football.

Index

All About the World Cup

Nick Hunter

Raintree is an imprint of Capstone Global Library Limited,
a company incorporated in England and Wales having its
registered office at 7 Pilgrim Street, London, EC4V 6LB –
Registered company number: 6695582

www.raintreepublishers.co.uk
myorders@raintreepublishers.co.uk

Text © Capstone Global Library Limited 2014
First published in hardback in 2014
Paperback edition first published in 2014
The moral rights of the proprietor have been asserted.

.... by Richard Parker and Tim Bond
Picture research by Hannah Taylor
Production by Vicki Fitzgerald
Originated by Capstone Global Library Ltd
Printed in and bound in China by Leo Paper Products .td

ISBN 978 1 406 26558 3 (hardback)
17 16 15 14 13
10 9 8 7 6 5 4 3 2 1

ISBN 978 1 406 26559 0 (paperback)
18 17 16 15 14 13
10 9 8 7 6 5 4 3 2 1

British Library Cataloguing in Publication Data
Hunter, Nick.
All about the World Cup.
796.3'34668-dc23
A full catalogue record for this book is available from the
British Library.

Acknowledgements
We would like to thank the following for permission to
reproduce photographs: We would like to thank the following
for permission to reproduce photographs: Getty Images
pp. 4 (Per-Anders Pettersson), 5 (GABRIEL BOUYS/AFP),
6 (ADALBERTO ROQUE/AFP), 7 (PIERRE-PHILIPPE
MARCOU/AFP), 8 (Bob Thomas/Popperfoto), 9 (Rolls Press/
Popperfoto), 10 (GIANLUIGI GUERCIA/AFP), 11 (Mario
Castillo/Jam Media/LatinContent), 12 (Richard Heathcote),
13 (Bob Thomas), 16 (Popperfoto), 17 (Ian Walton), 19
(Chris McGrath), 20 (Laurence Griffiths), 21 (AFP PHOTO /
KARIM JAAFAR), 22 (Cameron Spencer), 23 (FRANCISCO
LEONG/AFP), 26 (Stuart Franklin), 27 (Matthias Kern), 28
(Buda Mendes/LatinContent), 29 (Stuart Franklin/Bongarts);
Photoshot pp. 14 (Picture Alliance), 15 (Actionplus/Anthony
Stanley), 18 (Actionplus/GPA/Luca Ghidoni), 24 (Xinhua/Xu
Suhui), 25 (Offside/Talking/Mark Leech).

Cover photograph of Spain's national football team celebrating
winning the World Cup at Soccer City stadium in Soweto,
Johannesburg in 2010, reproduced with permission of Getty
Images (AFP PHOTO / JAVIER SORIANO).

Every effort has been made to contact copyright holders of
material reproduced in this book. Any omissions will be
rectified in subsequent printings if notice is given to the
publisher.

Disclaimer
All the internet addresses (URLs) given in this book were valid
at the time of going to press. However, due to the dynamic
nature of the internet, some addresses may have changed, or
sites may have changed or ceased to exist since publication.
While the author and publisher regret any inconvenience this
may cause readers, no responsibility for any such changes can
be accepted by either the author or the publisher.